TIPS FOR
VINTAGE STYLE

TIPS FOR VINTAGE STYLE

CATH KIDSTON

EBURY PRESS
LONDON

For Stanley

7 9 10 8

Published in 2004 by Ebury Press, an imprint of Ebury Publishing

A Random House Group Company

Text copyright © Cath Kidston 1999, 2004

Photographs copyright © Pia Tryde 1999

The Random House Group Limited Reg. No. 954009

Addresses for companies within the Random House Group can be found at
www.randomhouse.co.uk

A CIP catalogue record for this book is available from the British Library

The Random House Group Limited supports The Forest Stewardship
Council (FSC), the leading international forest certification organisation. All our titles
that are printed on Greenpeace approved FSC certified paper carry the FSC logo.
Our paper procurement policy can be found at www.rbooks.co.uk/environment

To buy books by your favourite authors and register for offers visit www.rbooks.co.uk

Printed and bound in China by C&C Offset Printing Co., Ltd

ISBN 9780091900380

contents

introduction

I love an element of surprise in design – the idea of,
say, using an old chintz fabric for a laundry bag or a
leftover piece of striped linen for a roller towel. An old
vintage dress fabric inspired my first ironing board
cover – and the idea proved so popular that many
more vintage style items, ranging from tablecloths and
seat cushions to tea towels, followed. The beauty of
vintage style is that it doesn't need to cost a lot – I
scour junk shops, flea markets and car boot sales
collecting fabrics, furniture and ideas along the way.

In this book I have attempted to distill the essence
of my first book, *Vintage Style*. My aim is not to create
a room that looks consciously designed but rather
a room that looks lived in, comfortable, fun and
welcoming. Welcome to my world.

KITCHEN

paint inspirations

Kitchens are the one room in the house that need to be repainted fairly regularly, and the most practical solution is to keep it simple by adding a fresh coat of white paint.

When choosing other colours, look to your kitchenware for inspiration. I have collected an enormous number of red and white bits and pieces over the years. There is everything from striped storage jars to chequered enamel pans, egg cups, soup ladles and mugs. So the other paint colours in my kitchen are shades of red.

When making a collection for your kitchen, It need not always be the patterns that match; it could purely be the colours. You are just as likely to find something modern in the high street as something older in a junk shop.

seat cushions

Kitchen chairs are so adaptable. You will find that by simply painting them to match your kitchenware you bring colour harmony to a room.

To make chairs instantly more comfortable, you can add squab seats. Try covering the seat cushions in matching or varied fabrics. Even better, you can have different patterns on each side of the cushions for easy changes. Squab seats are also easy to take off the chairs and wash.

Padded chairs can also be given a new lease of life using vintage fabrics. I especially like the effect of using the same pattern but different colourways.

the kitchen table

Finding the right size table for a room isn't always easy. If you need a larger table than your existing one, improvise with a large piece of wood from a timber merchant laid over the top. With a tablecloth thrown over the top no one need ever be any the wiser! This is also a great idea if you have a house full of people – at Christmas, for example – and need a larger table only occasionally.

To alter the feel of a room, change the tablecloth. Classic combinations that work well include brightly coloured red and white, blue and white, and yellow and white ginghams.

You can pick up vintage fabrics so easily: I garner them from all sorts of different places, such as thrift shops.

vintage fabrics

Vintage fabrics can make great tablecloths and if there are no other patterns in a room, big bold floral prints look great on a table – whether it's the kitchen, dining room or a small table in the sitting room.

It is possible to find them already made into curtains and so long as they are washable cotton and not interlined they are easy to convert.

Old curtains are often the right size for a 180cm (6ft) table and it is usually a case of just unpicking the heading tape and lining and hemming along one end.

floral tablecloth

If you find a beautiful piece of vintage floral fabric that is too small to use as a tablecloth, enlarge it!

1   Take an old linen sheet (or buy some new white linen or cotton) and cut it into four wide strips.

2   Stitch each strip to one edge of your chosen decorative fabric and to each other at the corners.

3   Hem the edges or, to add some more colour, finish the edges in a contrasting bias binding.

For the bias binding, choose one of the colours from the main piece of fabric. Or introduce a completely different colour for contrast, such as blue in a red kitchen. This works well because the different colour adds interest and variety.

tea towels

In addition to tablecloths and napkins, tea towels bring colour and interest to a kitchen. As they are often on full display, try to have cloths that look cheerful in the room.

Old floral towels from the 1950s look particularly good but they are quite hard to find and sometimes have frayed edges. Remedy this by trimming off the ends and adding a border, such as a strip of crocheted lace.

Lace is available in many widths and patterns, ranging from the simplest of triangles to more ornate designs.

It is easy to make your own colourful tea towels by hemming rectangles of printed linen. Edging the cloths with bias binding also looks good.

floral towel roller

One of my favourite things in the kitchen is an old floral towel hanging from a simple wooden roller painted white for a touch of freshness.

1   Make a towel for a roller by starting with a piece of thick cotton fabric. (I like to use material from vintage linen curtains.)

2   Line the fabric with white towelling, stitching the two pieces together, right sides facing. Turn the right way around and sew together the ends to finish.

A good way to decorate a larder is in a stark, practical manner, whitewashing it from top to toe. If your floor is concrete, you can whitewash this too. Fit as many shelves and storage cupboards as possible.

check tablecloth

Vintage fabrics work well in any room because just a small piece can be used to striking effect. To make a tablecloth, fit for any home:

1   Stitch two narrow pieces of vintage fabric to make a central runner for a tablecloth.
2   Add strips of a contrast design on each side. Gingham is perfect for a kitchen. You now have a custom-made table cloth.

For a coordinated kitchen, choose fabrics that feature similar colours but different patterns. Stripes and checks are my favourite. You can reverse the trend and choose fabrics with the same patterns but different colours.

ticking bags

Food doesn't always need to be stored in jars – ticking bags are also ideal for storing foods, as I discovered when I was given some herbs in a striped bag. This is also an excellent way to keep pulses and rice, and bags are just as easy to use as storage jars.

If you have a glass-fronted cupboard, make the most of it by using different fabrics in co-ordinated colours. They look really pretty all together behind the glass.

Small bags are perfect for using up miscellanenous pieces of fabric. Blue, red and white stripes and checks can all be used to great effect.

Label the bags by writing directly on to them or on to a piece of sticky tape with a laundry marker pen.

jam jar covers

Rather than using string or an elastic band, bright coloured hair scrunchies are great for attaching the fabric, and luggage labels are excellent for gift tags.

Alternatively, you can make your own tags from coloured card. Cut out with pinking scissors or cut into ad hoc shapes. A hole punch and some ribbon is then all you need for attaching them.

Home-made jam and marmalade make great presents but don't be deterred if you are not a keen cook. I am hopeless at making them, so I cheat and buy them from the local market! Or decant biscuits or sweets into glass jars, and finish them in the same way.

the kitchen apron

There are many attractive ways of adding colour to a kitchen using fabrics. Look for cheerful prints to use as:

- Tablecloths
- Tea towels
- Napkins
- Aprons.

This last come in a wide variety of shapes. You can still find incredible old pinnies in thrift shops and they come in the most wonderful prints.

Kitchen aprons are often very kitsch but are good fun and amusing to collect. I once had a great apron spelling out the calories of every conceivable food. When they are very colourful, they look great hanging up in the corner of the kitchen.

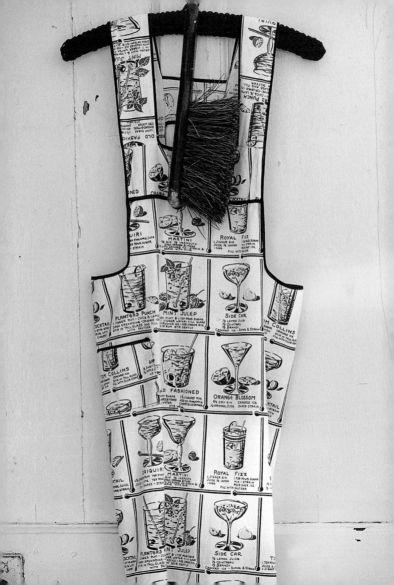

book jackets

Old cook books can be very entertaining. Besides the recipes, they often have great illustrations and very funny cookery pictures of the strangest combinations of food – roast chicken decorated with glacé cherries or a 'log' of gammon and pineapple, for example!

Cook books that are used regularly are best if they are covered in oilcloth or paper jackets as they can so easily be ruined.

1   Open a book out flat on the reverse side of your chosen paper. Draw around the edges, leaving a good 5cm (2in) margin.

2   Cut out the paper, trim triangles off the corners to make flaps for folding over the top, bottom and side edges and also to push into the ends of the spine.

3   Fasten in place with small pieces of sticky tape.

napkins

Use leftover fabric scraps, including tablecloth remnants, to make napkins. Don't worry about having matching napkins: assorted piles – such as ready-made red checked napkins mixed with ticking stripes and ginghams – look just as good.

It doesn't matter if you have only enough fabric for the odd napkin as this can be used to line, say, a bread basket.

Bias bindings make lovely edgings on napkins and tablecloths. This cotton tape is available in the most incredible colours and looks great when the different binding colours are allowed to clash.

food covers

A friend once made me a food cover out of a piece of old 1950s' kitchen fabric and she used an old broken necklace to weight the edges. The beads look positively jewel-like as well as being so practical.

Ricrac braid is an easy way to finish off a small circular hem as you don't have to turn over the fabric, which can be tricky.

An alternative would be to buy a ready-made braid with beads – stitch it on and, hey presto!

shopping bags

Shopping bags and baskets have a wide array of uses. French bread, for example, is good stored in a bag as the long loaves don't fit too well in a bread bin.

The baskets are also excellent for storing fruit and vegetables on the floor. They even come in handy as over-night bags. They are much more practical than using plastic bags, which always seem to burst.

You can make bags in a traditional tote shape out of printed upholstery fabrics or even from old plaid wool blankets. Line them with canvas to keep them strong. This is especially necessary if they are to be used to carry the shopping. Alternatively, line large wicker baskets with fabric.

LAUNDRY

cleaning

Above all else, a laundry or utility room has to be practical. Here are some ideas garnered from when I created my laundry area:

- If the entrance to your laundry is by the back door, lay a practical flooring such as lino, which is easy to keep clean.

- Install simple deep shelves for storing all those large items that amass in this room.

- A high shelf running around the room is very useful for storing flower vases and pots out of the way.

- A peg rail is helpful for hanging the ironed laundry.

- Towelling curtains work well in this room because it doesn't matter if they get wet. Leave them unlined and have ties at the top so they can be easily taken down and thrown in the wash.

tidying up

It is always worth hanging on to pieces of ribbon and trimmings as you never know when you will want to dress something up a little.

Keep old biscuit tins and glass jars and divide your trimmings among them. Perhaps sort them out by type or colour. This is a far more satisfactory way of looking after them, much better than rummaging through a larger box or trunk.

Wicker baskets are perfect for holding other items such as cleaning products, and enamelware buckets are great for storing all those messier items like the shoe-polishing kit. A peg rail is perfect for a collection of shopping bags – they are easy to gather on the way out.

the airing cupboard

If, as in my home, your airing cupboard has been built around the boiler, it will be the warmest space in the house. While this is just perfect for airing clothes and sheets, the room will need ventilating a little.

The best way to do this is to install doors with the top panels removed. Cover the panels with lengths of fabric fitted on to stretchy wire at the top and bottom. The end result is both pretty and practical as the curtains are easy to take down and wash.

Finish the inside of the cupboard with lots of simple slatted shelves so the piles don't become too deep and cumbersome.

Slats are the best form of shelving for an airing cupboard because the air circulates more easily.

doing the ironing

When I had my small flat, the ironing board was always on show in the kitchen. I was horrified by the choice of covers available in the shops so I converted a wonderful old floral curtain into a cover and it became part of the decoration.

Ensure you use a flameproof lining and check the fabric does not have any man-made content, which could be flammable. A heavyweight cotton lasts longer, too.

Trace the pattern from the old ironing board cover and finish it with a draw string so it's easy to wash.

Each time a cover wears out, it is simple to add a new one on top – the board gets more and more padded, too, which is an advantage!

coat hangers

Knitted coat hanger covers look wonderful. They are quick to make and use up lots of scraps of yarn. Knit reasonable widths of stripes and stitch around a padded hanger.

Alternatively, use scraps of leftover fabric and add fabric flowers for extra decoration. If you don't have your own collection of remnants, you can always find them in department stores. Satin and vintage designs look especially good.

It is easiest to cover a coat hanger that is already padded. Pin the fabric so its seam runs across the top, which can then be hand stitched.

peg bags

One of the essential items for a washing line is a peg bag – I made mine from a piece of printed dress fabric.

1   Cut out two pieces of fabric the same shape.

2   Trace the outline of a wooden coat hanger for the top and make the bag narrower in the middle so the pegs don't fall out in the wind.

3   Leave an opening on one side and edge this with some bias binding for a neat and colourful finish. A little matching bow stitched at the top is a charming addition.

A bag like this is easy to make and could also be used as a good general storage bag.

smelling good

Keep your laundry smelling good in the airing cupboard by tucking lavender bags in between the blankets.

Scented bars of soap also keep the moths away. They give a wonderful smell to the room as a whole and are a great alternative to the rather musty smell of mothballs.

You can use up all sorts of scraps and ribbons to make lavender bags, even cutting up old items of clothing such as shirts and nightdresses.

Don't feel restricted to making squares – circles and rectangles are just as good. Finish each one with a ribbon tie. It is possible to make piles of them in an evening and they are great gifts.

ribbon ties

It is very practical to keep pairs of sheets tied together in your linen cupboard. It can be hard to tell what size a sheet is once it is put away, so to save the bother of opening them up to find out, use different coloured ribbons to represent single or double when putting away the sheets. As long as they are loosely tied, the ribbons can be recycled.

If you prefer to keep your sheets separate or don't use them in pairs, coloured ribbons come in very handy once again. Stitch a short length of ribbon to the end of each sheet and ensure when you fold the sheet after ironing that it always shows. You might choose to always use, say, green for single sheets and lilac for double.

SITTING ROOM

practical comfort

If a sofa needs reupholstering, you might prefer to think of using a loose cover instead. These are especially practical if you have children and animals to contend with: sticky fingers and muddy paws often leave a trail over the furniture.

If you find a piece of fabric that you particularly like but it isn't large enough to cover the whole sofa, consider using it just to cover the seat cushions.

This is especially effective if you want to use a stronger colour but worry that it is too much for a whole cover. Even more simply, you could just tuck the material around the cushions – easy to take off and clean and then throw back on again.

chair covers

When the covers of your chairs are worn out, don't buy a new one, simply disguise what you have.

One of my armchairs needed a loose cover to cover its rather sickly velvet upholstery. Some pink and red ticking went well, but there wasn't nearly enough so I patched the back with another fabric. Rather than try to match it, I used a clashing piece of Moroccan striped awning cotton.

If the upholstery of a sofa or armchair is still in reasonable condition but looking a little jaded, throw brightly coloured rugs over the back to add some extra or up-to-date colour.

paint choices

Simple decor in the sitting room works so well as the main colours can be off-set by something a little more different.

Introduce vibrant colours in small quantities by painting, say, a small piece of furniture in the colour of your choice.

Be inspired by your furnishing fabrics or a favourite painting. I often choose paint colours from the coloured bindings of cloth books. They come in the most fantastic shades and it is much easier to take a book to the paint store and have the colour matched than it is to choose from one of those tiny swatches.

patchwork patterns

Patchwork upholstery on sofas and armchairs looks just fantastic. Patchwork also has the benefit of using up a collection of small amounts of fabric.

As long as the essential element – variations on plaid patterns, say, or different shades of the same colour – remains the same, you can use a wide variety of fabrics.

Use any leftover pieces for cushion covers. Using different designs on each side of the cushion – for example a bold chintz on one side and striking plaid on the other – means you have double the decorative choice.

Chintz and ticking work together well too. These witty combinations prevent a room from being too serious, and the cushions also add to the cosiness factor.

perfect schemes

For a more contemporary setting, paint your sitting room white and leave the floorboards bare. Bleaching the boards will make the room look even more sophisticated.

Once you have chosen other colours for the room, keep a look out for objects that will enhance your scheme. Working with such a narrow choice of colours means that even the smallest of items will look lovely.

For example, any piece of wooden furniture can be painted to suit the room. Or small pieces of fabric can be turned into a tablecloth, cushion cover or a runner for a mantelpiece. The end result is a room that has been lovingly and carefully thought about.

extra seating

Kids' chairs are great assets for any room. Use them as side tables and if they are armless they can also come in handy for extra seating. They are easy to tuck away in a corner, ready to bring out in an emergency.

Old school chairs are easy to find in natural wood, but are quickly and readily transformed to whatever colour you choose with a plain coat of paint.

For a more aged look, choose colours that have a faded air to them and once the paint is dry, attack the furniture with sandpaper. Don't be shy about this part of the operation – the more haphazard you are, the better.

Look for waterbased paint because it is softer and so easier to remove for a 'weathered' effect.

clashing shades

Trimmings are an especially easy way to add a little extra to a cushion cover: tour around your local haberdashers and you will soon find lots of items.

Bias bindings are great value for this purpose and are readily available in a huge range of colours and widths.

Buttons and braids are other simple ways of adding colourful interest to cushion covers.

I like to add bias binding to the edge of a cushion and a bow is a practical closure. If you cannot find an exact match for something, consider using a completely clashing colour instead – the contrast is always a little surprising and adds a bit of life to a room.

flower power

Flowers make a huge difference in a sitting room. Besides adding colour and scent, they make a house feel alive and lived in.

Try to mix together a few clashing colours – say three shades of pink or a jumble of orange and pink – and simply pile them into a jug or vase.

Alternatively, buy just one variety but a mass. Cheap carnations, for example, look great in a huge bunch.

Simple country blooms, such as snapdragons, lilies and roses, always look lovely together, no matter how different their colours.

patchwork blankets

Fantastically colourful patchwork blankets are readily collectible and have myriad uses. They are easiest to find in charity shops or flea markets.

The best ones have crocheted edges and truly wicked colour combinations. Besides using them as the more conventional blanket or throw they also convert into excellent cushion covers or dog rugs.

They can be formed from stripes that are pieced together with simpler, plain sections or small squares sewn together in a more regular fashion.

Whatever patchwork blanket you find or decide to make, their charm lies in their colourfulness and informality. They are just perfect for curling up under next to a roaring log fire.

chintz

Of all the vintage fabrics, chintz is the most versatile.
I just love the abundance of the designs and the
robustness of the colours.

The fabric works especially well as small sections in
tablecloths and as cushion covers.

Or use a larger piece as a cloth on a side table draped
over a more understated piece of fabric that puddles
onto the floor.

Boldscale chintz makes great cushions on a modern
sofa – a huge splash of print on a plain cover. The
cushions need to be large.

candle power

If you are having a party, it is lovely to light the room
with lots of candles, be they in antique candlesticks
reflected by the mirror or tiny night lights dotted
around the place.

Candlesticks positioned in front of a mirror are
especially effective because their reflection gives you
double the light. Candlesticks incorporating glass and
beads are especially pretty when lit by a mirror.

Be careful where you put your candles – particularly if
there are a lot of people milling around. Position them
as high as possible or within high-sided containers.
Night lights in painted glass jars, for example, are
effective – and safe.

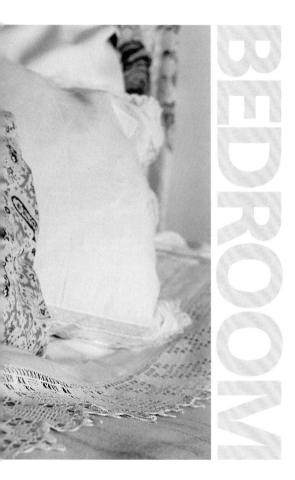

BEDROOM

modern florals

There can be a tendency with some old-fashioned floral fabrics for the room to end up looking like it belongs to a very old lady. To avoid this, dress up the room with some contemporary colours.

Casually fold a brightly coloured throw or quilt across the end of the bed.

Change this depending on the season: something warm and inviting for the winter, in, say, rich purple or green; and a paler, lighter colour for the spring and summer – think sugared almond shades.

Checked blankets also do more than a little to address the potential fuddiness problem.

customized fabric

The lilac, green and white colour scheme of my bedroom stemmed from an oil painting of mauve hydrangeas left to me by my aunt, which I like very much. I also had a set of engravings with old-fashioned green mounts.

With this sort of inspiration, you can set out to look for material for curtains. If you can't find exactly the right shade, consider having a fabric printed in the colourway of your choosing.

There are a few companies that will print their designs to any colour. If you print enough it will not cost much more than usual. You will need to be confident in your fabric so that you can feature it large in your bedroom, perhaps using it for curtains, valance and bedhead.

window seats

A window seat can be a great addition to any room.

Make cushion covers from left-over curtain fabric or other pieces you might have.

Consider introducing a few different colours of fabric to help lift the space. It helps to inject some extra colour into a room, because if everything matches too closely it can look rather contrived.

Bobble fringing or other similar textured trimming adds yet more interest and variation.

Hang white muslin curtains behind the main ones. The translucent curtains can be pulled closed on sunny days to soften the light.

linen sheets

Linen sheets and old-fashioned blankets have to be the most inviting of bedding choices. Plain white linen is the best and is relatively easy to find. The best linen comes from Ireland and is beautiful but hugely expensive. Vintage linen often comes up for sale at auctions.

Look for pretty antique pillowcases decorated with lace and mix these with patterned ones. Also look for antique sheets – transform plain ones by sewing heavy cotton lace on to their edges.

Add a warm and comforting blanket and then top it all with a pile of cushions covered with your favourite fabrics, perhaps with the occasional lacy trim.

making lampshades

Old lampshades often have far more character than the ones available now and it is easy to find them in junk shops. Even if they are covered in some hideous fabric, you can have them re-covered in your own favourites.

My delicate organza lampshade was made by stitching striped organza carefully on to an old wire frame. Lampshade frames can be bought new, too.

1   Gather the fabric around the top of the frame and stitch into place.

2   Attach to the bottom of the frame in the same way.

3   To cover the stitching and finish off the lampshade, sew on a frill over both top and bottom.

the guest room

A peg rail is a practical and attractive addition to a guest room. It's perfect for hanging up clothes and is better than installing a wardrobe as so much more space is left in the room.

Leave some pretty covered coat hangers on the rail to add to the decoration (see page 50) – and to encourage guests to use it.

If at all possible, ensure there is space for a comfortable chair is in this room so that your guests feel even more at home. You can't have too many cushions on it. It is no problem if they don't match the rest of the decor. In fact, for such small items, the more clashing the better.

real bedding

Making a traditional bed with sheets and blankets is a particular favourite of mine. It is just so lovely climbing into a bed made up like this and especially welcoming to visitors.

For a good old-fashioned style of bedding, use candy-striped cotton sheets with matching pillowcases. They are still made in all sorts of colours. To finish off, pile a mixture of quilts and blankets on top.

If you like to continue a decorative theme throughout a room, don't forget to include pictures in your planning. Even postcards work well – if you have a large mirror, tuck them into the frame.

feather quilts

I love collecting old feather eiderdowns. They come in the prettiest faded paisley prints and really do keep you warm.

It is hard to find them in good condition but they can be successfully cleaned in the washing machine and put through the tumble dryer, which often helps. Check there are no holes first or you can end up with feathers everywhere.

The other option is to re-cover an old beaten-up eiderdown in a loose cover, making the equivalent of a duvet cover, and edge it with a small silk taffeta frill and ties. Some dry-cleaners will still re-cover eiderdowns in your own fabric.

recycled blankets

A hot-water bottle ready on cool evenings and biscuits by the bed along with the clean linen sheets are very inviting for your guests.

1   Make a hot-water bottle cover by cutting two pieces of an old woollen blanket slightly larger than your bottle.

2   Turn under the edges and then stitch together around three sides.

3   On the remaining seam attach lengths of ribbon, which are used to tie the cover over the hot-water bottle.

Blanket makes a wonderful hot-water bottle cover as it ensures the water stays hot for as long as possible. Ribbons are a pretty addition and also a great way to use up some left-over scraps.

dyed sheets

I like to dye pretty antique sheets all sorts of different colours and then use them as bed covers.

Old linen sheets take dye very well and it is fun to mix the pretty colours of the top and bottom sheets on the bed. They work best if they are made from pure linen and if they are dyed in pale pastel shades in the washing machine.

New linen sheets are extremely expensive to buy but it is easy to pick up old ones in antique markets at a good price.

So your bed looks even prettier, make pillowcases from floral prints and trim the blanket with the same fabric.

final details

It can be great fun choosing suitable items for any room of the house. In the guest room, think about including any of the following:

- The latest magazines by the bed.
- A cosy flannel dressing gown to hang on the back of the door.
- Fluffy towels in various sizes. Be generous, include the largest bath towel you can find.
- Colourful vases filled with flowers, ready for the arrival of your guests.

These ideas form just as much of the decoration as anything else. Furthermore, it is details like these that can add so much to the finished effect.

comfort blankets

It is easy to buy old wool blankets these days as so many people choose to use duvets instead. They are one of the best bargains in second-hand shops and good quality ones will usually wash well.

On cold winter nights, the weight of a blanket or two is most comforting, especially if you are lying between newly laundered sheets that smell of fresh air.

For warmer nights, fold your blanket back to the end of the bed ready for pulling back over the bed in the morning. If you want to add extra colour to a room, casually throw one of your favourites across the bed.

lacy pillowcases

There are all sorts of pillowcases that I like to use to decorate my beds.

For example, look for some pretty dress-making fabrics in linen and brushed cotton, which make up well into covers. They look really pretty edged with haberdashery lace and are very easy to make. I mix them up with plain white or coloured linen sheets.

For something a little less fancy, white cotton or linen makes crisp pillowcases. Make your own or search for old linen ones – they are remarkably easy to find. You will find them with and without lace additions.

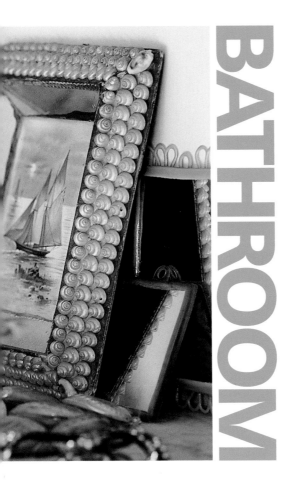

BATHROOM

firelight

An original fireplace in the bathroom can make a lovely focal point. Not only can you relax in the bath but you – and other people – can also take time out in armchairs cosily positioned on each side of the fire. Try covering bathroom chairs with towelling fabric – it's practical and turns the chair into a great place for hair drying and relaxing,

If your bathroom is spacious enough, include a wardrobe, which is always useful for storing bulky towels.

An even better addition, if there's space, is a freestanding coat stand, for hanging up dressing gowns and towels.

scenic fabrics

To keep a bathroom as airy as possible, paint it a cream-coloured off-white and and paint the woodwork a pale shade of 'French' grey to soften the effect. If it faces out on to the street, install louvred shutters at the windows for privacy.

Such a neutral backdrop is perfect for dressing up with small finds. For example, I used a small amount of 1950s' scenic boat fabric to make some cushions and a squab seat for the chairs in my bathroom.

I also had a baby deck chair that I couldn't resist covering to add to the seaside atmosphere of the room. Now it sits comfortably by the fireplace.

washbags

All sorts of material can be used to make washbags – so long as they are washable.

1   From some white cotton or towelling, make a bag with a wide hem at the top and a small gap in the side seams near the bottom of the hem. Run a line of stitching 2.5cm (1in) from the top and thread ribbon through the hem beneath the line.

2   Cut out a picture or part of a pattern from any scraps of fabric you might have.

3   Appliqué the picture to the washbag with small, neat hand stitches.

If you choose the right fabric these bags can look great hanging from a bathroom shelf.

shell pictures

Mantelpieces are perfect for displaying your favourite treasures. Choose a themed display or an eclectic mix, or perhaps just have one or two of your best pieces.

In my bathroom I have a collection of Victorian seaside pictures with shell frames I wanted to use. I was concerned that using shells to decorate the bathroom was a bit of a cliché so, rather than hang the pictures, they all sit stacked along the mantelpiece.

Mixed among them is a collection of colourful plastic mirrors from Morocco.

As you come across items, add them to your display, nestling them among what's there already.

vintage towelling

You can buy towelling in all sorts of colours plus it is also available with patterns on it. Choose your favourite and customize it to make your own towels and flannels by edging it with bias binding.

Bias binding is available in different widths and, of course, very many colours. Use vibrant combinations of colours to reflect the colours in the fabric or the towelling's design.

Ring the changes, too, by using contrasting thread to stitch the bias binding in place. White can looks very effective against a dark coloured background, especially if the towelling is white. The white stitching makes a virtue of the bias binding and, of course, unifies it still more with the white towelling.

bathroom splashes

As bathroom fittings are predominantly white, add splashes of colour to the room.

Look for colourful pieces of fabric (I have used the perfect piece of floral fabric with bunches of lilac, pink and yellow flowers on a fresh white background) to cover the seats of any chairs in the room.

Choose fluffy, colourful bath mats and towels. Towels look lovely on display so keep them neatly folded in an open shelving unit.

Soaps are made in so many delicious colours that they too are a fun way of establishing a colour theme. Store them in a large glass jar so you can enjoy them even when not in use.

hand towels

There are all kinds of hand towels around in markets and junk shops that are perfect for brightening up a spare bathroom. Or run up your own using old fabric.

1   Make hand towels from scraps of linen. This needn't be plain fabric, prints work just as well.

2   Cut out a single layer of linen and make a narrow hem at each side.

3   Add an edging of heavy cotton lace at each end.

These towels look so pretty and they are also very easy to wash, dry and press, ready for the next guest.

You can buy your lace new or remove it from old, worn-out sheets and pillowcases.

glass jars

Fill glass jars gathered from around the house with different-coloured bubble baths and cotton wool balls to line the shelves of your bathroom.

The jars look good when they are grouped together, particularly when they are put on a window sill with the light streaming through.

The advantage of decorating a room like this is that the end result is bright and airy and it is very simple to put together.

- Huge glass sweet jars are handy for storing bath toys or makeup.
- A jam pot is perfect for cotton wool buds.
- Old glass decanters look especially pretty when they are filled with different coloured bubble baths.

keeping clean

The smallest items can be used to introduce wit and colour to the bathroom. Keep your eye open for useful – and perhaps unusual – additions that complement your decorative scheme, such as coloured bottles, bubblebath and soaps.

I have a collection of nailbrushes in many novelty shapes and colours. You can find these in my bathroom. I have a pair in lime green and fuchsia pink which are old favourites.

To accompany them, I knitted a cleaning cloth from matching pink cotton. It didn't take long and the end result is great – combining function with some fun!

kelim chair

In this picture you can see many of the elements that I think make for the perfect, comfortable bathroom.

Having the space for at least one chair in a bathroom is luxury indeed – a great place to relax.

A carpet underfoot adds comfort to those bare feet and the thick fluffy towelling robe means you stay warm and cosy at all times – both before and after your bath.

Having a sunny bathroom is a joy and louvred windows means that you can continue to enjoy the light but at the same time retain that all-important sense of privacy.

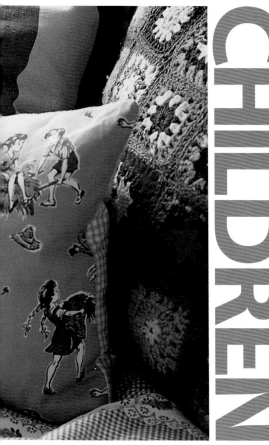

CHILDREN

girls' room

Take your inspiration for the decoration of a room from anything – curtain fabric, a picture – anything goes.

To create impact with an unusual design, use a single strip of a favourite fabric in each curtain and add gingham borders on each side.

Colour coordinate the room by using more of the main design to cover a toy box or make some cushions.

Other places to use the fabric might include:

- The glass panels of the door
- Shoe or toy bags
- As a cloth over the bedside table.

cushions

A child's bed covered with a mixture of cushions means that it can also be used as a sofa.

I love brightly coloured woollen crochet blankets and enjoy making them into cushion covers. Because crochet and knitted fabrics don't keep their shape especially well it is always worth making the reverse side of a woollen cushion cover out of cotton or linen.

Make other cushion covers from scraps of old ticking or gingham and also use some of the curtain material.

If you are going to have lots of different fabrics, aim to link them through colour or pattern alone. Too great a mixture can be chaotic.

bold and bright

I like to pick up old furniture in junk shops and then paint it in bright colours. Nothing is then too precious and it doesn't really matter if it gets broken, which is, of course, always useful in a child's bedroom.

Oilcloth fabric makes a practical and cheerful covering in a child's room. It's a perfect work top as children can paint on it and create all sorts of other mess and it's easy to wipe clean.

It is a fabric that also comes in handy when a baby comes to stay. I have an old table to which I have stapled a piece of oilcloth which makes a great changing table.

fabric touches

Don't feel that you have to stick to paint when it comes to a spot of redecorating. Fabric works well too for toyboxes, cushions, pictures and more.

I even have an old Moses basket that I revamped using a favourite print.

It's easy to create children's bed linen to coordinate with their room:

1   Make sheets from white flannel and trim them with some fabric used elsewhere in the room. You might prefer to use a different colourway for variation.

2   In a third colourway of the same design, stitch a new slip cover for the quilt with a pillowcase to match.

gingham

Gingham is a good addition to any room and it can be especially successful in a bedroom.

Used by itself for curtains or in combination with other fabrics, the effect is striking and yet also friendly.

Gingham also looks good used in smaller details:

- Stitched onto a lampshade
- As part of a patchwork quilt
- As a pillowcase. Use the gingham either for the

whole cover or as a trimming such as for covering a button closure or as ribbon ties.

Don't forget that gingham comes in masses of different colourways, not just the typical red and white.

covered sofa

If you have the space, an old sofa is a perfect addition in a child's room. If yours needs covering, make a suitable sized blanket from some polar fleece. This is such great fabric for children. It is softer than cashmere, cheap and easy to wash.

Bind the edge of the cover in gingham and perhaps add some embroidered motifs to continue any theme you may have chosen for the room's general décor.

Cutting out images from material and appliquéing them to cushion covers can be another successful way of furthering a theme.

To enhance the charm of such cut-outs, appliqué them in a higgledy-piggledy fashion.

contrasting fabrics

Adding a squab seat and cushion to a small wooden chair is a charming addition to a child's bedroom. I like to use piping on cushion and squab covers because it gives them such a professional finish. You can buy piping ready made in all sorts of different colours but if you want it to match your fabric you are going to have to make it yourself. It is suprisingly easy.

1   Cut 2.5cm (1in) wide strips of your chosen fabric on the bias (diagonally across the grain).

2   Sew the strips together to make the necessary length.

3   Pin the strips around plain piping cord, right side out, and stitch as near to the cord as you can.

painted finishes

Never underestimate the versatility of paint. Not only is it available in whatever colour you choose, it is quick to apply, the effect is immediate and if it chips – quite likely in a child's room – it can be touched up instantly. For your instant brightening, paint:

- Picture frames to reflect its content or your chosen colour theme
- Cheap pieces of furniture; either single colours or pick out details with contrasting lines or more zany patterns
- Metal bed heads with enamel
- Floorboards.

Remember always to prepare your surface thoroughly to ensure there is enough grip for the paint to adhere to. Wash the surface very well too.

fabric pictures

There is no reason why you shouldn't create your own pictures using pieces of material you have used elsewhere in the bedroom or playroom. This is obviously most successful if the fabric design is pictorial.

1　Cut out the parts of the fabric that you would like to use as a picture. Leave a good 5cm (2in) border around the image.

2　Measure the area of each image – only the part that will ultimately be on display.

3　Cut plywood to these measurements. Stretch the fabric over the front and staple it in place on the back of the mount.

4　Add some string to the back of the picture using small 'D' rings for hanging.

knitting

Knitted toys are often for sale in a local market and make great gifts for new-born babies in particular (although I know one ten-year-old who is still pretty much besotted with her collection). The patterns are still available in knitting shops, too, and are an excellent way of using up ends of balls of wool. Be careful not to add plastic eyes or buttons or anything similar that could be pulled off and swallowed.

If you like knitting, it is possible to find great designs for hand-knitted cardigans with motifs such as Scottie dogs, ducks and sheep. With a little planning, these patterns are easy to convert into knitted cushion covers. They don't have to be large covers; in fact, one or two smaller ones look very charming at the end of a bed or cot.

raffia embroidery

Raffia embroidery is remarkably simple to do. Coloured raffia is quite easy to come by and simple designs can be quickly and effectively created using a blunted embroidery needle with a large eye. Keep an eye out for old craft books as they often have good designs in them that are easy to copy.

Raffia embroidery works especially well on a Moses Basket. You don't have to buy one that is ready-made although you should buy a special, breathable baby's mattress. Lining the basket is not difficult because you can stitch the fabric to the edge fairly easily – as long as you have strong fingers and/or a thimble.

toy boxes

Old ottomans are great as toy chests. On the one in my home I have used an old velvet curtain to upholster the sides so that it will better withstand wear and tear. To make the padded top:

1   Attach a thick layer of wadding to the top of the lid with glue.

2   Cut a piece of cream lining material that is large enough to cover the top, sides and tuck under the lid. Stretch over the wadding and fasten with a staple gun to the underside of the lid.

3   Repeat with the covering fabric, making neat tucks at the corners.

4   For a neat finish, cut a piece of the covering fabric to fit the underside plus seam allowances. Fold under allowances, and pin and stitch the fabric in place.

HOME OFFICE

creative comforts

It your workplace is really an extension of the main sitting and entertaining room and used by all the family, you will want to retain its domestic atmosphere but somehow incorporate the efficiency of a proper office.

Hide your desk in a corner, away from the main part of the living room. If you don't need masses of desk space, look for something a little more informal rather than using a full scale piece of office furniture.

Add some simple floor-to-ceiling book shelves and house your filing among the books.

Finally, I spend a good deal of time on research, browsing through books and magazines, and I reckon an armchair – if not a sofa – is vital for this. If you have the space, put one into your office space too.

creating order

An old desk with pigeon holes is wonderful for keeping post and paperwork in order. Under the desk keep a filing system in stacks of box files, each covered in a different paper or fabric.

Use each box for a different subject, such as one for bank statements and one for the car documents. With their different coverings they are instantly recognisable. Filing like this is so much easier than in a proper filing cabinet as, if information needs to be taken elsewhere, the whole box can be carried around.

Clothes pegs instead of paper clips are also good for tidying up paperwork. Keep a huge box of brightly coloured plastic ones on the desk for this purpose.

coloured chalk board

For messages and notes prop up a chalkboard in your working area.

You'll find it just as practical as a blackboard and if you change the colour it won't remind you of school.

So long as the colour is fairly intense to ensure that the chalk is clearly visible, these boards look great in all sorts of colours. Use an oil-based paint with a matt finish.

It is so practical, it would be worth putting one in the kitchen, too, for all those shopping lists and reminders of things to do for the whole family.

storage solutions

An old wire post office rack is completely perfect for filing and storage. It is especially good for stationery as the wire boxes are exactly the right size for piles of blank paper and everything is clearly visible. Although my desk is always cluttered, the sight of all my writing paper and envelopes neatly stacked on the shelves along with the receipt books at least gives the appearance of an efficient work place.

Cardboard boxes can also be a very functional form of storage. You can buy or order good sturdy ones with lids from packaging companies. They come in all sorts of sizes and are incredibly cheap.

You can leave them a natural cardboard colour but they also look very smart painted or covered in fabric.

scrubbed pine

It is good to work in natural light as much as possible so set up a table close to a window. Install a phone point together with a bank of plugs to service the area.

My desk is really an old kitchen table. I chose it because it has an adjustable top and is not too work-like. It extends when I need to spread myself out, but normally it is kept folded down.

If you want something similar, look for one made of pine, which can be scrubbed down and bleached. This makes it very hard-wearing and impervious to all those hot mugs of coffee and tea

Keep the computer printer underneath the table where it is out of sight but convenient to use.

book shelves

Book shelves close to a desk are extremely useful. You need to have as many of them as possible – have them reaching from ceiling to floor – and designed with various heights of book in mind.

It can be helpful, too, to have them divided into shorter lengths of shelf as this helps keep your books looking neat and tidy.

Keep all your practical reference books on these shelves, organized so that the ones you use most regularly are on the shelf nearest to where you sit.

The ones that I use the most are also bound in different fabrics and papers (for advice on how to do this, see page 33).

freshly bound

I began by covering telephone directories with paper and fabric and then moved on to such items as my address book, message book and atlas. It has become quite a habit!

Not only are they much more easily identifiable in their jackets, but they also withstand wear and tear much more readily.

This can be a great way of using up old scraps of wallpapers and fabric – stick them on with spray glue.

To make a special present for someone, cover a favourite read or blank notebook with velvet or damask and add a ribbon so that it can be tied shut.

pin boards

A noticeboard is incredibly practical in a work place as it can be used for pinning up all sorts of things, ranging from lists and photos to stamps and even the odd cheque waiting to be banked.

1   Buy or cut a large piece of pin board.

2   Wrap it in tin foil or fabric, stapling it to the back.

3   Stretch a grid of black elastic over the top and staple this down where the lines cross.

I tried to make my board as decorative as possible and began by pinning up old prints and family photographs. The tin foil is now only visible in small chinks around the paperwork, but when the afternoon sunshine floods into the room the light is beautifully reflected from it.

vintage fabrics

I love these vintage abstract fabrics but I can often only find short lengths these days. They are becoming very collectible so I am careful not to cut them up to make such small items as cushion covers or napkins.

Instead, frame your favourites on plain canvas stretchers and hang them grouped together or alongside some contemporary paintings.

The colours of these fabrics usually include plenty of primary shades so they make a very striking centrepiece on a wall. Use them, too, as inspiration for a colour scheme or to add some contrast.

cath kidston stores

Cath Kidston Marylebone

51 Marylebone High Street

London W1U 5HW   Tel: 020 7935 6555

Cath Kidston Chelsea Green

12 Cale Street

London SW3 3QV   Tel: 020 7584 3232

Cath Kidston Holland Park

8 Clarendon Cross

London W11 4AP   Tel: 020 7221 4000

Cath Kidston Fulham

668 Fulham Road

London SW6 5RX   Tel: 020 7731 6531

Cath Kidston New York (scheduled to open in Spring 2004)

201 Mulberry Street

New York, NY 10012

stockists

There are Cath Kidston stockists throughout the UK,
and worldwide. To find your nearest call:

Cath Kidston Head Office on +44 (0)20 7221 4248

visit the website: www.cathkidston.co.uk

email: info@cathkidston.co.uk.

To request a catalogue call: +44 (0)20 7229 8000.

visit the website: www.cathkidston.co.uk

email: mailorder@cathkidston.co.uk

index

about the author

Cath Kidston began her career working with Nicky Haslam and set up her own shop in London ten years ago. Her business has grown to four shops in London, a flourishing mail order business, and outlets worldwide. This spring her first store in New York will open. She sells her own bed linen, soft furnishings, fabric and wallpapers, as well as a broad range of accessories. Her designs feature regularly in leading magazines.